I0408914

Table of Contents:

Chapter 1: Introduction to Dumpster Diving

What is Dumpster Diving?

Dumpster diving is the practice of retrieving discarded items from dumpsters, often for personal use, recycling, or reselling. It is a form of urban scavenging that has gained popularity due to its potential for saving money and reducing waste. Dumpster divers search for items such as food, clothing, furniture, electronics, and other household goods that have been thrown away by individuals, businesses, or institutions.

At its core, dumpster diving is a way to make use of items that are still functional and valuable but have been discarded for various reasons. These items may include surplus inventory, slightly damaged goods, expired food items, or items that have been replaced or upgraded. Dumpster divers see the potential in these discarded items and aim to give them a second life.

The History and Culture of Dumpster Diving

While dumpster diving has become more popular in recent years, its roots can be traced back to various movements and cultures throughout history. During periods of economic downturn, dumpster diving has often been seen as a survival strategy. In times of scarcity, individuals have turned to dumpsters as a means of finding necessities.

In recent decades, dumpster diving has also gained traction as a way to protest against consumerism and waste. Activists and environmentalists have embraced dumpster diving as a form of direct action to raise awareness about the consequences of excessive consumption and to promote resourcefulness and sustainability.

In addition to its historical context, dumpster diving has also developed its own subculture. There are online communities, forums, and social media groups dedicated to sharing tips, experiences, and finds from dumpster diving expeditions. Dumpster divers often form supportive networks, exchanging information about fruitful locations, sharing stories of successful dives, and offering encouragement to fellow divers.

Misconceptions and Stigmas Surrounding Dumpster Diving

Despite its growing popularity and the benefits it offers, dumpster diving is not without its fair share of misconceptions and stigmas. Many people hold negative assumptions about dumpster diving, associating it with poverty, dirtiness, or illegal activities. It is important to address and debunk these misconceptions to provide a more accurate understanding of dumpster diving.

First and foremost, it is essential to recognize that dumpster diving is not synonymous with homelessness or destitution. While some individuals may engage in dumpster diving as a means of survival, many others do it as a choice, seeking to reduce waste, save money, or find unique items. Dumpster diving is practiced by people from various backgrounds, including students, artists, environmentalists, and those looking to supplement their income.

Another common misconception is that dumpster diving is illegal. While laws regarding dumpster diving vary from place to place, it is generally legal to retrieve discarded items from public dumpsters. Private property and trespassing laws, however, must be respected. It is important for dumpster divers to familiarize themselves with the specific regulations in their area to ensure they are diving within the boundaries of the law.

Furthermore, dumpster diving does not necessarily involve digging through piles of filth and garbage. With careful selection and an understanding of the best locations to dive, it is possible to find items in clean and sanitary conditions. Dumpster divers often take precautions such as wearing gloves, using hand sanitizer, and inspecting items carefully before taking them.

By dispelling these misconceptions and addressing the stigmas associated with dumpster diving, it becomes easier to appreciate the benefits and possibilities that this activity offers. Dumpster diving can be a rewarding and sustainable practice that allows individuals to save money, reduce waste, and discover unexpected treasures.

Chapter 2: The Joys of Dumpster Diving

Dumpster diving is not just a means to an end; it can also be a source of joy, fulfillment, and even a way of life. In this chapter, we will explore the various aspects that make dumpster diving a truly enjoyable experience.

Dumpster Diving as an Interesting Job

One of the unique aspects of dumpster diving is that it can be a job in itself. For some individuals, dumpster diving is their primary source of income. They have honed their skills, developed a deep understanding of the best diving locations, and mastered the art of finding valuable items. These individuals may work as independent divers, selling their finds online or at flea markets, or they may even establish their own thrift stores.

The Flexibility of Dumpster Diving as a Part-Time or Full-Time Gig

One of the advantages of dumpster diving as a job is its flexibility. Unlike traditional employment, dumpster diving allows you to set your own working hours. This flexibility can be especially beneficial for those who have other commitments, such as students, parents, or individuals pursuing other entrepreneurial ventures. Whether you want to dive for a few hours a week or make it a full-time pursuit, dumpster diving offers the freedom to tailor your schedule to your needs.

Setting Your Own Working Hours and Taking Breaks

As a dumpster diver, you have the autonomy to decide when and how long you want to work. You can choose to dive early in the morning, late at night, or whenever it suits your schedule. If you need a break, you can simply take one without having to seek permission or adhere to strict schedules. This level of control over your working hours can provide a sense of freedom and independence that is often lacking in traditional employment settings.

The Freedom and Enjoyment of the Lifestyle

Beyond the financial aspect, many individuals find joy in the lifestyle that dumpster diving offers. It allows you to break free from the consumerist mindset and find satisfaction in repurposing discarded items. Dumpster diving encourages resourcefulness and creativity, as you repurpose or refurbish items to give them new life. This process of transforming trash into treasure can be immensely fulfilling and enjoyable.

Moreover, dumpster diving provides a sense of adventure and exploration. Each dive is like a treasure hunt, filled with the anticipation of discovering valuable or unique items. It takes you to unexpected places, introduces you to diverse communities, and allows you to connect with fellow divers who share your passion. The thrill of uncovering hidden gems and the satisfaction of finding something of value can bring immense joy and a sense of accomplishment.

In conclusion, dumpster diving offers more than just a way to save money, it can be an interesting job, a flexible gig, and a lifestyle that brings joy and fulfillment. The freedom to set your own hours, the excitement of the hunt, and the satisfaction of repurposing discarded items contribute to the overall enjoyment of dumpster diving. Whether you dive for financial reasons, environmental concerns, or simply for the thrill, the joys of dumpster diving make it a unique and rewarding pursuit.

Chapter 3: The Treasure Trove: What You Can Find

Dumpster diving is like entering a treasure trove of discarded items. From food to clothing, furniture to household items, and even valuable collectibles, the range of items that can be found while diving is vast. In this chapter, we will delve into the various categories of items you can discover through dumpster diving and explore their potential value.

Exploring the Various Items You Can Find While Dumpster Diving

When it comes to dumpster diving, the saying "one person's trash is another person's treasure" holds true. The items you can find vary greatly depending on the location and type of dumpsters you explore. Supermarkets, retail stores, residential areas, and even construction sites can yield an array of discarded items.

Food is one category that often surprises people. Supermarkets and restaurants frequently discard edible items that are nearing their expiration dates but are still perfectly safe to consume. Fruits, vegetables, packaged goods, and even bakery items can be found in abundance. Many dumpster divers have been able to significantly reduce their grocery bills by rescuing perfectly good food from going to waste.

Clothing is another treasure often discovered in dumpsters. Retail stores, donation centers, and even residential areas may discard clothing that is slightly damaged, out of season, or simply unwanted. With a bit of cleaning and mending, these items can be transformed into stylish and wearable pieces. Some divers even stumble upon vintage clothing or designer labels, making their finds all the more exciting.

Furniture and household items are commonly discarded by people moving, downsizing, or upgrading their homes. Couches, chairs, tables, lamps, and various other home furnishings can be found in dumpsters near residential areas or apartment complexes. With a little TLC, these items can be restored to their former glory or repurposed creatively.

The Potential Value of Discarded Items

While dumpster diving offers the opportunity to find practical and functional items, it can also lead to valuable discoveries. Antiques, vintage items, and collectibles are often discarded without the knowledge of their true worth. By developing an eye for unique and valuable items, dumpster divers have stumbled upon rare finds such as antique furniture, vintage clothing, old records, or valuable artwork.

Electronics and jewelry are other categories that can hold significant value. Electronic devices such as smartphones, tablets, or gaming consoles may be discarded due to minor defects or when newer models are released. Jewelry, whether lost or discarded, can be discovered in unexpected places. Dumpster divers have found valuable pieces such as gold, silver, or gemstone jewelry, which can fetch a substantial price if sold or traded.

Uncovering Hidden Gems That Could Be Worth a Significant Amount

One of the thrills of dumpster diving is stumbling upon hidden gems—items that hold unexpected value or have a unique appeal. These hidden gems can vary widely and are often found when least expected. From rare books and vintage vinyl records to original artwork and limited-edition items, the possibilities are endless. These discoveries can not only provide a sense of excitement but also become valuable assets or collectibles.

It is important to note that while dumpster diving can yield valuable items, not every dive will result in a significant find. The true value lies in the combination of small savings, practical items, and occasional treasures. The thrill of the hunt and the satisfaction of repurposing discarded items can be just as rewarding as the monetary value.

Recycling Metals and Making Money from Scrap Yards

In addition to finding usable items, dumpster divers can also profit from recycling metals. Many discarded items contain metals such as aluminum, copper, or steel, which can be recycled and sold to scrap yards. Items like cans, wires, or appliances that contain metal components can be dismantled and recycled, providing a source of income while promoting sustainability.

By recycling metals, dumpster divers contribute to reducing waste and the demand for extracting raw materials. It is a win-win situation that benefits both the environment and the divers themselves.

In conclusion, dumpster diving reveals a treasure trove of items across various categories, from food and clothing to furniture and household goods. While practicality and savings are key benefits, dumpster diving can also lead to valuable discoveries such as antiques, collectibles, electronics, jewelry, and hidden gems. Additionally, recycling metals found during dives provides a sustainable and profitable avenue. The world of dumpster diving is full of surprises, offering not only financial savings but also the thrill of uncovering treasures and making a positive impact on the environment.

Chapter 4: Dumpster Diving Legality

Dumpster diving exists in a legal gray area, as laws and regulations surrounding the practice can vary depending on the jurisdiction. In this chapter, we will explore the legal aspects of dumpster diving, including federal, state, county, and city laws, as well as considerations regarding private property and trespassing laws.

Federal Laws Regarding Dumpster Diving

At the federal level, there are generally no specific laws that explicitly prohibit dumpster diving. However, certain laws related to privacy, property rights, and waste disposal may indirectly impact the practice. For example, the Fourth Amendment protects individuals from unreasonable searches and seizures, but it does not extend the same protection to discarded items in public spaces.

State, County, and City Laws

Laws regarding dumpster diving can vary significantly from one state, county, or city to another. It is important to research and understand the local laws in your area before engaging in dumpster diving.

Understanding Private Property and Trespassing Laws

One crucial aspect to consider when dumpster diving is the issue of private property and trespassing laws. Dumpsters located on private property, such as those belonging to businesses or residential complexes, may require permission from the property owner before accessing them. Trespassing laws vary, and individuals found trespassing on private property without permission may face legal consequences.

Navigating Legalities to Stay Within the Boundaries

While dumpster diving may be legal in some cases, it is crucial to navigate the legalities to ensure that you are within the boundaries of the law. Here are some considerations to keep in mind:

1. Research Local Laws: Familiarize yourself with the specific laws and regulations regarding dumpster diving in your jurisdiction. This may involve consulting municipal codes, contacting local authorities, or seeking legal advice if necessary.

2. Public vs. Private Property: Distinguish between dumpsters located on public property, such as those on the street or in public parks, and those on private property. Accessing dumpsters on private property without permission may be considered trespassing, so it is important to seek proper authorization.

3. Respect Posted Signs: Pay attention to any signs or notices posted near dumpsters that indicate whether access is allowed or restricted. Some businesses may explicitly prohibit diving, while others may have specific guidelines for use.

4. Exercise Caution and Common Sense: Use common sense and exercise caution when engaging in dumpster diving. Avoid situations that may lead to legal trouble, such as damaging property, causing a disturbance, or engaging in illegal activities while diving.

It is important to note that the information provided here is a general overview and should not be considered legal advice. Laws and regulations can change, and specific circumstances may require consulting legal professionals to ensure compliance with local laws.

By understanding the legal aspects of dumpster diving and adhering to applicable laws and regulations, divers can mitigate the risk of legal consequences and engage in the practice responsibly.

Chapter 5: Maximizing Your Dumpster Diving Haul

Dumpster diving not only allows you to find valuable items but also presents an opportunity to make the most of your finds. In this chapter, we will explore strategies for sorting out your discoveries, evaluating their value, and maximizing your haul through various avenues such as selling, donating, gifting, or repurposing.

Sorting Out Your Finds: What to Keep, Sell, Donate, Gift, or Throw Away

After a successful dive, it is essential to sort through your finds and determine what to keep, sell, donate, gift, or discard. This process involves assessing the condition, functionality, and personal value of each item. Consider factors such as practicality, sentimental attachment, and market demand when making decisions.

Items that are in good condition and fulfill a personal need can be kept for personal use. These may include clothing, household items, or furniture that can enhance your daily life. By keeping items you need, you reduce the need for purchasing them new, thereby saving money and reducing waste.

Evaluating and Valuing Your Discoveries

To maximize the potential value of your finds, it is crucial to evaluate and value each item. Research similar items online or consult with experts in specific categories to assess their market value. Factors such as condition, rarity, brand, and desirability can affect the perceived value of an item. Accurately valuing your discoveries allows you to make informed decisions when it comes to selling or trading them.

Selling Items on Online Platforms like eBay, Etsy, and Craigslist

One popular avenue for monetizing your dumpster diving finds is by selling them on online platforms such as eBay, Etsy, and Craigslist. These platforms provide access to a large customer base and allow you to reach potential buyers worldwide. Take high-quality photos, write detailed descriptions, and set competitive prices to attract buyers and maximize your chances of a successful sale.

Starting Your Own Thrift Store or Selling at Flea Markets

If you have a considerable number of items to sell, you may consider starting your own thrift store or participating in local flea markets. This allows you to create a physical presence for your business and interact directly with customers. With careful curation, attractive displays, and fair pricing, you can establish a reputation and attract loyal customers who appreciate the value of your finds.

It is important to research local regulations and obtain any necessary permits or licenses before starting a thrift store or participating in flea markets. Compliance with zoning laws, health regulations, and taxation requirements is essential to operate legally and avoid potential legal issues.

Donating to Charitable Organizations or Those in Need

Items that are in good condition but may not hold significant resale value can be donated to charitable organizations or individuals in need. Local shelters, community centers, or organizations that support vulnerable populations often accept donations of clothing, furniture, and household items. By donating your finds, you contribute to the well-being of others and help reduce waste.

Selling Bulk Items or Exporting Goods for Profit

If you have a large quantity of specific items, you may explore the option of selling in bulk or exporting goods for profit. Some buyers, such as vintage clothing wholesalers or overseas distributors, may be interested in purchasing items in bulk. Research potential buyers, negotiate fair prices, and ensure that all legal requirements for exporting goods are met.

By diversifying your approach and considering various avenues for maximizing your haul, you can turn dumpster diving into a profitable venture. Remember to adhere to local laws and regulations regarding selling, trading, and exporting goods to ensure a legal and ethical practice.

Chapter 6: Essential Tools and Preparation

To embark on a successful dumpster diving journey, it is crucial to have the right tools and be prepared for the adventure ahead. In this chapter, we will explore the essential equipment needed for dumpster diving, discuss protective gear and safety tips, and provide guidance on ideal timeframes and locations for successful dives.

The Equipment You Need to Start Dumpster Diving

While dumpster diving may seem like a low-cost activity, having the right equipment can significantly enhance your experience and ensure your safety. Here are some essential tools you should consider having:

1. Gloves: Sturdy gloves will protect your hands from sharp objects, broken glass, or potential contaminants.

2. Flashlight or Headlamp: A reliable light source is essential for exploring dumpsters, especially in dimly lit areas or during nighttime dives.

3. Grabber Tool: A grabber tool or a long-reaching tool can help you retrieve items from deep within dumpsters without having to physically climb in.

4. Bags and Containers: Durable bags or containers are essential for carrying your finds. Opt for reusable bags or bins that can withstand the weight and protect the items.

5. Folding Cart or Dolly: A folding cart or dolly can be useful for transporting larger or heavier items from the dumpster to your vehicle.

6. Cleaning Supplies: Keep some cleaning supplies handy to clean and sanitize items you find, especially if you plan to sell or donate them.

Protective Gear and Safety Tips

Dumpster diving can involve potentially hazardous conditions, so taking precautions and wearing appropriate protective gear is essential. Consider the following safety tips:

1. Wear Closed-Toe Shoes: Protect your feet from sharp objects or broken glass by wearing closed-toe shoes or boots.

2. Dress Appropriately: Wear long-sleeved shirts and pants to protect your skin from scratches, cuts, or potential contaminants.

3. Use Hand Sanitizer: Keep a small bottle of hand sanitizer with you to maintain hygiene after diving and before handling food or personal items.

4. Stay Alert: Be aware of your surroundings and any potential dangers, such as unstable or overflowing dumpsters, slippery surfaces, or hostile animals.

Ideal Timeframes and Locations for Successful Dives

Choosing the right time frames and locations for dumpster diving can significantly impact your success. Consider the following factors:

1. Store Closing Times: Dive shortly after stores close to increase your chances of finding fresh, discarded items.

2. Collection Days: Research the collection schedules in your area to determine the best days to dive. Generally, the night before or the morning of collection days can yield fruitful results.

3. Seasonal Considerations: Different seasons may affect the availability of certain items. For example, the end of the school year or holiday seasons often leads to an increase in discarded items that can be found near student residences or retail stores.

4. Explore Diverse Locations: Expand your search beyond retail stores to include residential areas, apartment complexes, universities, restaurants, or construction sites.

Each location may offer unique opportunities for valuable finds.

Being Prepared with Essentials like Gloves, Bags, and a Flashlight

Before heading out on a diving expedition, ensure you are fully prepared with all the essentials. Double-check that you have your gloves, bags, flashlight or headlamp, and any other necessary equipment. It is also a good idea to bring a fully charged mobile phone for emergencies and to let someone know your diving plans for safety purposes.

By equipping yourself with the right tools, wearing protective gear, and being prepared for various diving scenarios, you can enhance your safety and overall experience. Always prioritize your well-being and adhere to local laws and regulations while engaging in dumpster diving.

Chapter 7: Ups and Downs of Dumpster Diving

Dumpster diving is an adventure that comes with its fair share of ups and downs. In this chapter, we will explore the joys and challenges of dumpster diving, discuss how to embrace the unpredictability, overcome obstacles, celebrate successes, and build resilience in the pursuit of finding hidden treasures.

Embracing the Unpredictability of Dumpster Diving

One of the exciting aspects of dumpster diving is the element of surprise and unpredictability. Each dive is unique, and you never know what you might find. Embrace this sense of adventure and keep an open mind as you explore different dumpsters.

Remember that not every dive will result in valuable discoveries, but the anticipation and possibility of finding something special make the journey worthwhile.

Overcoming Challenges like Bad Weather and Unproductive Days

Dumpster diving is not always smooth sailing. There will be days when the weather is unfavorable, making diving uncomfortable or even impossible. Rain, snow, extreme heat, or cold can pose challenges and affect the condition of items in the dumpsters. Additionally, there may be unproductive days when you come across fewer or no valuable finds. It's important to stay positive and not let these challenges discourage you. Use unproductive days as an opportunity to explore new locations or take a break and recharge.

Celebrating Successes and Learning from Failures

When you find a valuable item or have a successful dive, take a moment to celebrate your achievement. It's important to acknowledge and appreciate the rewards that come with dumpster diving. At the same time, it's equally important to learn from failures or less fruitful dives. Not every dive will be a success, and that's okay. Reflect on what went wrong or what you could do differently in the future to improve your chances of finding valuable items.

Building Resilience and Perseverance in the Pursuit

Dumpster diving requires resilience and perseverance. It takes time, effort, and patience to become skilled at spotting valuable finds and navigating the challenges that come

with practice. Building resilience means staying motivated, even when faced with setbacks or unproductive dives. Remind yourself of the financial savings, environmental impact, and the joy of finding hidden treasures that come with dumpster diving. Surround yourself with supportive individuals who understand and appreciate your passion for this unique endeavor. Developing a positive mindset, focusing on the thrill of the hunt, and celebrating both big and small successes will help you stay resilient and motivated as a dumpster diver, because each dive is an opportunity to learn, grow, and enjoy the adventure, regardless of the outcome.

Chapter 8: Safety and Ethics in Dumpster Diving

Dumpster diving, like any activity, requires attention to safety and ethical considerations. In this chapter, we will explore the importance of practicing good hygiene, handling potentially hazardous materials, respecting expiration dates, and being a responsible member of the dumpster diving community.

Hygiene Practices and Precautions

Maintaining good hygiene is crucial when engaging in dumpster diving. Here are some important hygiene practices and precautions to follow:

1. Wear Gloves: Always wear protective gloves when diving to avoid direct contact with potentially dirty or contaminated items.

2. Use Hand Sanitizer: Carry a small bottle of hand sanitizer and use it frequently to keep your hands clean and free from germs.

3. Wash Hands Thoroughly: After each diving session, wash your hands with soap and water to ensure cleanliness.

4. Avoid Food Contamination: If you find edible items, carefully inspect them for signs of spoilage or contamination.

When in doubt, it's better to err on the side of caution and discard potentially unsafe food.

Handling Potentially Hazardous Materials

While dumpster diving, you may come across items that can be potentially hazardous to your health or safety. It's important to exercise caution when handling such materials:

1. Chemicals and Cleaning Products: Be cautious when handling chemicals or cleaning products found in dumpsters. Avoid direct contact and use protective gloves if necessary.

2. Broken Glass or Sharp Objects: Watch out for broken glass, sharp objects, or other hazards that can cause injuries. Always wear appropriate footwear and use tools like a grabber to avoid direct contact.

3. Biological Waste: Exercise caution if you come across medical waste or biological materials. These items should not be handled without proper training and disposal procedures.

Respecting Expiration Dates and Avoiding Spoiled or Unsafe Items

When finding food items, it is crucial to respect expiration dates and avoid consuming spoiled or potentially unsafe items. Check the labels and packaging for expiration dates, signs of spoilage, or any damage that may compromise the safety or quality of the product. It is essential to prioritize your health and well-being when deciding whether to keep or discard food items.

Being a Responsible Member of the Dumpster Diving Community

Dumpster diving is a shared activity, and it is important to be a responsible member of the diving community. Here are some considerations:

1. Clean Up After Yourself: Leave the diving area clean and tidy after you finish. Dispose of any trash or unwanted items properly and avoid leaving a mess behind.

2. Respect Private Property: Adhere to property rights and avoid trespassing on private property without permission. Always seek authorization before accessing dumpsters located on private premises.

3. Share Information Responsibly: While it's great to share diving tips and information with fellow divers, be mindful of disclosing sensitive or confidential details about specific locations or businesses. This helps protect the integrity of the practice and maintains a respectful relationship with local establishments.

By practicing good hygiene, handling potentially hazardous materials with care, respecting expiration dates, and being a responsible member of the dumpster diving community, you can engage in the activity safely and ethically. Remember that responsible diving not only ensures your own well-being but also helps maintain a positive image of dumpster diving as a sustainable and valuable practice.

Chapter 9: Beyond Personal Gain: Sharing and Giving Back

While dumpster diving can be a way to save and make money, it also presents an opportunity to go beyond personal gain and make a positive impact on others. In this chapter, we will explore ways to assist those in need with your dumpster finds, gift treasures to friends and family, sell bulk items or export goods for profit, and create a broader positive impact through dumpster diving.

Assisting Those in Need with Your Dumpster Finds

One of the most fulfilling aspects of dumpster diving is being able to help those who are less fortunate. Consider donating usable items, such as clothing, furniture, or household goods, to local charities, shelters, or community organizations. These organizations can distribute the items to individuals or families in need, providing them with essential resources and improving their quality of life.

Gifting Friends and Family with the Treasures You Discover

When you come across unique or valuable items during your dives, consider gifting them to friends and family. Sharing your finds not only brings joy to loved ones but also reduces waste and promotes sustainable consumption. Pay attention to their interests and needs, and choose items that align with their preferences. Your thoughtful gifts can be a pleasant surprise and may even inspire others to explore the possibilities of dumpster diving.

Selling Bulk Items or Exporting Goods for Profit

If you come across a significant quantity of specific items during your dives, you may consider selling them in bulk or exporting goods for profit. Some buyers, such as thrift stores, vintage clothing wholesalers, or overseas distributors, may be interested in purchasing items in larger quantities. Research potential buyers, negotiate fair prices, and ensure compliance with any legal requirements related to selling or exporting goods.

Creating a Positive Impact through Dumpster Diving

Dumpster diving can have a broader positive impact beyond individual gains. Consider the following ways to create a positive influence through your dumpster diving activities:

1. Environmental Awareness: Raise awareness about the environmental impact of excessive waste and consumerism by sharing your experiences and knowledge with others. Encourage sustainable practices such as recycling, upcycling, and reducing waste.

2. Education and Advocacy: Share information about the benefits of dumpster diving, including reducing waste, saving money, and finding unique treasures. Educate others about the legality and ethics of the practice to combat misconceptions and stigmas associated with it.

3. Community Outreach: Get involved in community initiatives that promote sustainability, such as local recycling programs, environmental cleanup efforts, or educational workshops on reducing waste. Share your dumpster diving experiences and insights to inspire others to take action.

By assisting those in need, gifting treasures to friends and family, selling items in bulk, and creating a broader positive impact through education and community involvement, you can make a meaningful difference beyond personal gain. Dumpster diving becomes not only a way to save and make money but also a means to contribute to a more sustainable and compassionate society.

Chapter 10: The Thrill of the Hunt: Valuable Discoveries

One of the exciting aspects of dumpster diving is the possibility of finding valuable items amidst discarded materials. In this chapter, we will explore the thrill of the hunt and discuss how to identify valuable items during dumpster diving, recognize unique finds like antiques and collectibles, understand the potential value of electronics and jewelry, and uncover hidden gems that could be worth a significant amount.

Identifying Valuable Items during Dumpster Diving

Developing an eye for valuable items is a skill that comes with experience and knowledge. Here are some tips to help you identify valuable items during your dives:

1. Research and Education: Stay informed about current trends, market values, and popular collectibles. Read books, magazines, and online resources related to antiques, vintage items, and other valuable goods. Attend workshops or join online forums to learn from experts and fellow enthusiasts.

2. Visual Inspection: Practice a keen sense of observation. Look for signs of quality, craftsmanship, and brand names

when examining items. Take note of unique features, signatures, or markings that may indicate value.

3. Condition and Rarity: Consider the condition of the item. Items in excellent condition or with limited availability are generally more valuable. Look for items that are in demand but scarce in the market.

Unique Finds: Antiques, Vintage Items, and Collectibles

Dumpsters can sometimes yield treasures from the past. Antiques, vintage items, and collectibles have the potential to be highly valuable. Keep an eye out for:

1. Antique Furniture: Look for well-crafted furniture pieces made from high-quality materials. Items with unique designs or historical significance can be particularly valuable.

2. Vintage Clothing and Accessories: Pay attention to vintage clothing, handbags, shoes, and accessories. Designer labels, iconic styles, or limited edition pieces can fetch a high price in the vintage fashion market.

3. Collectible Items: Be on the lookout for items that are highly sought after by collectors, such as coins, stamps, trading cards, or comic books. Research popular collectible categories and familiarize yourself with valuable items within those niches.

Recognizing the Potential of Electronics, Jewelry, and Other High-Value Items

Dumpsters can be a source of valuable electronic devices, jewelry, and other high-value items. Consider the following:

1. Electronics: Look for electronics such as smartphones, tablets, laptops, or gaming consoles. Test them if possible to ensure they are in working condition.

2. Jewelry: Keep an eye out for discarded jewelry, including necklaces, bracelets, earrings, or rings. Precious metals like gold or silver, as well as gemstones, can significantly contribute to their value.

3. Art and Decorative Items: Dumpster diving can yield art pieces, sculptures, or decorative items. Research artists, art movements, and popular styles to determine potential value.

Uncovering Hidden Gems that Could Be Worth a Significant Amount

Sometimes, valuable items may not be immediately recognizable. Train yourself to look beyond the obvious. Consider the following:

1. Research and Appraisal: If you suspect an item might be valuable but are unsure, seek professional appraisal or

consult experts in the respective fields. Their expertise can help you identify hidden gems.

2. Unusual or Niche Items: Keep an eye out for items that may have niche or specialized markets. Unique items, oddities, or items from specific historical periods can attract collectors and enthusiasts willing to pay a premium.

3. Potential for Restoration or Repurposing: Items that may appear damaged or worn out at first glance could have value if they can be restored, repaired, or repurposed. Consider the potential value after investing time and effort into restoring or transforming the item.

Developing an understanding of valuable items takes time and practice. With research, education, and experience, you can sharpen your eye for valuable finds and increase your chances of discovering hidden gems during your dumpster diving adventures.

Chapter 11: Growing as a Dumpster Diver

Dumpster diving is a journey of continuous learning and growth. In this chapter, we will explore the importance of experience and continuous learning in dumpster diving, discuss how to build relationships with fellow divers, share knowledge, tips, and tricks within the community, and expand your expertise while honing your dumpster diving skills.

The Importance of Experience and Continuous Learning

Experience plays a significant role in becoming a skilled dumpster diver. The more dives you undertake, the more familiar you become with different locations, the patterns of waste disposal, and the types of items commonly discarded. Through experience, you learn to spot valuable finds more efficiently and develop a sense of intuition about where to focus your efforts. Embrace each dive as an opportunity to learn and grow, building on your knowledge with every new find.

Continuous learning is equally important in dumpster diving. The practice is ever-evolving, and there is always something new to discover. Stay updated on trends, techniques, and industry developments by:

1. Reading Books and Resources: Explore books, guides, and online resources dedicated to dumpster diving. Learn from the experiences and insights of seasoned divers who have shared their knowledge in writing.

2. Following Online Communities: Join online forums, social media groups, and discussion boards dedicated to dumpster diving. These communities provide a wealth of information and support.

3. Attending Workshops or Seminars: Look for workshops, seminars, or conferences related to recycling, sustainability, or upcycling. These events can provide valuable insights and connections within the dumpster diving community.

Building Relationships with Fellow Dumpster Divers

Building relationships with fellow dumpster divers can greatly enhance your experience and growth in the field. Connect with others who share your passion by:

1. Joining Local Groups: Seek out local dumpster diving groups or create your own. These groups allow you to meet like-minded individuals, share experiences, and explore diving opportunities together.

2. Participating in Meetups: Attend local meetups or organized diving events to connect with divers in your area.

These gatherings provide opportunities to share tips, learn from others, and foster a sense of community.

3. Engaging Online: Interact with fellow divers through online communities, social media groups, or dedicated forums. Share your finds, seek advice, and offer support to others. The online space allows for networking and learning from divers across different regions.

Sharing Knowledge, Tips, and Tricks within the Community

Sharing knowledge within the dumpster diving community is a valuable practice that benefits everyone involved. By freely exchanging information, tips, and tricks, you contribute to the growth and improvement of the community. Consider:

1. Contributing to Online Discussions: Participate in online discussions by sharing your experiences, insights, and discoveries. Offer advice to newcomers and learn from the experiences of others.

2. Organizing Skill-Sharing Sessions: Arrange skill-sharing sessions or workshops within your local diving community. Share your expertise on specific topics, such as finding valuable items, navigating legalities, or maximizing profits.

3. Collaborating on Projects: Collaborate with fellow divers on projects that benefit the community or promote sustainability. This can include organizing community clean-up events, creating educational materials, or advocating for responsible waste management practices.

Expanding Your Expertise and Honing Your Dumpster Diving Skills

As you gain experience and knowledge, consider expanding your expertise in related areas. This can complement your dumpster diving skills and open up new opportunities. Some areas to explore include:

1. Sustainability and Upcycling: Learn about sustainable practices, upcycling techniques, and creative ways to repurpose found items. This knowledge can enhance the value of your finds and contribute to a more environmentally conscious lifestyle.

2. Recycling and Waste Management: Deepen your understanding of recycling processes, waste management practices, and local regulations. This knowledge will help you navigate the legalities and responsibilities associated with dumpster diving.

3. Business and Entrepreneurship: Consider developing skills in areas such as online selling, marketing, or running a small

business. This can empower you to turn your dumpster diving finds into profitable ventures, such as selling items on e-commerce platforms or starting your own thrift store.

By valuing experience, embracing continuous learning, building relationships with fellow divers, sharing knowledge within the community, and expanding your expertise, you can grow as a dumpster diver. With each dive, you become more knowledgeable, skilled, and connected to a network of passionate individuals who share your enthusiasm for this unique pursuit.

Chapter 12: The Freedom and Fulfillment of Dumpster Diving

Dumpster diving offers more than just financial savings, it provides a sense of freedom, self-sufficiency, and fulfillment. In this chapter, we will explore the aspects of embracing a life of freedom and self-sufficiency through dumpster diving, finding fulfillment in the art of diving, balancing financial savings with personal enjoyment, and encouraging others to explore the possibilities of dumpster diving.

Embracing a Life of Freedom and Self-Sufficiency

Dumpster diving allows you to break free from traditional consumerism and embrace a more alternative lifestyle. By salvaging discarded items, you reduce your dependence on buying new goods and contribute to reducing waste. Dumpster diving offers:

1. Financial Freedom: By finding useful items for free or at a significantly reduced cost, you can save money and allocate your resources to other areas of your life that matter most to you, such as travel, education, or personal goals.

2. Environmental Consciousness: Dumpster diving aligns with sustainability values by reducing the demand for new products, conserving resources, and diverting usable items

from landfills. This conscious choice contributes to a healthier planet and a greener future.

Finding Fulfillment in the Art of Dumpster Diving

For many divers, dumpster diving goes beyond practicality—it becomes an art form and a way to express creativity. The thrill of the hunt, the satisfaction of finding valuable items, and the joy of repurposing and upcycling provide a unique sense of fulfillment. Consider the following aspects:

1. Creativity and Resourcefulness: Dumpster diving inspires creative thinking and problem-solving as you repurpose found items in innovative ways. It taps into your resourcefulness, allowing you to see the hidden potential in discarded objects.

2. Personal Achievement: Each successful dive and valuable find contributes to a sense of accomplishment and self-worth. The process of transforming discarded items into useful or beautiful objects can be deeply satisfying.

Balancing Financial Savings and Personal Enjoyment

While dumpster diving offers financial savings, it's essential to strike a balance between frugality and personal enjoyment. Consider the following:

1. Setting Personal Goals: Determine your financial goals and aspirations. Allocate the money saved through dumpster

diving to areas of your life that bring you joy and fulfillment, whether it's travel, experiences, or personal projects.

2. Enjoying the Process: Embrace the joy of diving itself, rather than solely focusing on the financial benefits. Appreciate the adventure, the discoveries, and the learning experiences that come with each dive.

Encouraging Others to Explore the Possibilities of Dumpster Diving

Share your dumpster diving experiences with others to inspire them to explore this unique practice. By raising awareness and dispelling misconceptions, you can encourage others to consider dumpster diving as a viable option for saving money, reducing waste, and finding hidden treasures. Consider:

1. Education and Advocacy: Educate others about the benefits, legality, and safety of dumpster diving. Address common misconceptions and stigmas associated with the practice. Share your success stories and the positive impact it has had on your life.

2. Leading by Example: Be a role model by demonstrating responsible diving practices and ethical behavior. Show others how dumpster diving can be done safely, respectfully, and in harmony with the community and the environment.

By embracing a life of freedom and self-sufficiency, finding fulfillment in the art of diving, balancing financial savings with personal enjoyment, and encouraging others to explore the possibilities of dumpster diving, you can experience a profound sense of satisfaction, contribute to a sustainable lifestyle, and inspire others to embark on their own diving adventures.

Chapter 13: Dumpster Diving Cautions and Considerations

While dumpster diving can be a rewarding and exciting activity, it's important to be aware of potential cautions and considerations. In this chapter, we will explore how to navigate community attitudes towards dumpster diving, understand local laws and regulations, handle hazardous materials responsibly, and be mindful of expiration dates and potential health risks.

Navigating Community Attitudes towards Dumpster Diving

Dumpster diving is still stigmatized in some communities. Consider the following:

1. Privacy and Property Boundaries: Respect the privacy of individuals and businesses. Avoid diving in areas where you may be infringing on someone's personal space or private property. If in doubt, seek permission from property owners or seek out public areas where diving is allowed.

2. Discretion and Cleanliness: Practice discretion while diving to avoid drawing unnecessary attention. Clean up after yourself, leaving the diving location as clean as or cleaner

than you found it. This helps to foster a positive image of dumpster divers within the community.

Local Laws and Regulations to Be Aware Of

Laws and regulations regarding dumpster diving can vary by location. It's crucial to understand and abide by the rules in your area. Consider the following:

1. Legal Boundaries: Research federal, state, county, and city laws regarding dumpster diving. Familiarize yourself with any restrictions or regulations that may apply to your specific area. Be aware of laws related to trespassing, private property, and local ordinances.

2. Permissible Diving Locations: Some municipalities or businesses may prohibit or restrict diving in certain areas. Respect these restrictions and focus your efforts on locations where diving is permitted and legal.

Handling Hazardous Materials Responsibly

Dumpsters can contain hazardous materials that require proper handling to ensure your safety and the safety of others. Take the following precautions:

1. Protective Gear: Wear appropriate protective gear, such as gloves, sturdy shoes, and clothing that covers your body, to minimize the risk of injury or contamination.

2. Hazardous Waste: Be cautious of dumpsters that may contain potentially hazardous materials, such as chemicals, sharp objects, or biohazardous waste. Avoid direct contact with these items and do not attempt to handle or remove them.

Being Mindful of Expiration Dates and Potential Health Risks

When diving for food or other perishable items, it's crucial to be mindful of expiration dates and potential health risks. Follow these guidelines:

1. Expiration Dates: Inspect food items carefully and check for expiration dates. Use your judgment and common sense when determining the safety of food products. When in doubt, it's best to err on the side of caution and discard items past their expiration dates.

2. Hygiene Practices: Practice good hygiene habits when handling food or personal care items found in dumpsters. Wash your hands thoroughly with soap and water or use hand sanitizer after handling items.

3. Allergies and Dietary Restrictions: Take note of any potential allergens or dietary restrictions when diving for food. Respect these considerations and avoid sharing or consuming items that may pose a risk to yourself or others.

By navigating community attitudes, understanding local laws and regulations, handling hazardous materials responsibly, and being mindful of expiration dates and potential health risks, you can engage in dumpster diving with safety, respect, and consideration for others. These cautions and considerations will help you maintain a positive image of dumpster divers and ensure a safe and enjoyable diving experience.

Chapter 14: Great Dumpster Diving Locations

Finding the right dumpster diving locations is crucial for maximizing your chances of discovering valuable items. In this chapter, we will explore various types of locations that are known to yield fruitful dives. From supermarkets and shopping centers to residential areas and construction sites, we will cover a range of potential hotspots for dumpster diving.

Supermarkets and Grocery Stores

Supermarkets and grocery stores can be excellent places to find a variety of items, particularly in their dumpsters designated for perishable goods. Consider the following:

1. Produce and Bakery: Check dumpsters behind supermarkets for discarded fruits, vegetables, baked goods, and dairy products. Often, these items are still in good condition and can be salvaged for personal use or donation.

2. Non-Perishable Items: Some supermarkets dispose of non-perishable items like packaged foods, canned goods, and dry goods. These can be great finds for stocking your pantry or donating to local food banks.

Shopping Centers and Retail Stores

Dumpsters near shopping centers and retail stores can provide a diverse range of items. Explore these locations for potential treasures:

1. Clothing and Accessories: Many retail stores dispose of unsold or damaged clothing, shoes, and accessories. Check dumpsters behind fashion retailers, thrift stores, and department stores for discarded items that can be cleaned, repaired, or repurposed.

2. Electronics and Appliances: Retailers selling electronics and appliances sometimes dispose of returned or damaged items. Check dumpsters near electronics stores, home improvement stores, or appliance retailers for potential finds. Ensure that you follow safety precautions when dealing with electronics.

Residential Areas

Dumpsters in residential areas can be a treasure trove of various items. Keep an eye out for the following opportunities:

1. Moving and Spring Cleaning: As people move or declutter their homes, they often discard furniture, household items, and appliances. Explore dumpsters near apartment complexes, student housing, or residential neighborhoods during moving seasons or after large community events.

2. Curbside Pickup: Some municipalities have curbside pickup for bulk items or specific types of waste on designated days. Check local regulations and schedules to identify the best times to visit these areas for potential finds.

Construction Sites and Businesses

Construction sites and businesses can offer unique opportunities for dumpster diving. However, be mindful of safety and legality when approaching these locations:

1. Construction Materials: Construction sites may dispose of excess building materials, such as lumber, tiles, or hardware. These items can be repurposed for personal projects or sold for profit.

2. Businesses with Discarded Inventory: Some businesses, such as furniture stores, home improvement centers, or even bookstores, may discard inventory or display items that are no longer needed. Check dumpsters near these businesses for potential valuable finds.

It is always good to practice respect for private property, abide by local laws and regulations, and ensure your personal safety when exploring dumpster diving locations. With careful consideration and a keen eye, you can uncover hidden treasures in unexpected places.

Chapter 15: Organizing Your Finds

Once you've completed a successful dumpster diving expedition and gathered an assortment of items, it's important to have a system in place to organize and manage your finds effectively. In this chapter, we will explore strategies for sorting and categorizing your haul, storage solutions for different types of items, and tips for managing your inventory to stay organized.

Sorting and Categorizing Your Dumpster Diving Haul

Sorting and categorizing your finds is essential for easy access and efficient management. Consider the following strategies:

1. Grouping by Item Type: Sort your items into categories such as clothing, electronics, household items, furniture, or personal care products. This approach allows you to locate specific items quickly.

2. Prioritizing: Within each category, prioritize items based on their condition, value, or usefulness. This will help you identify which items to focus on first for cleaning, repairs, or selling.

3. Creating Subcategories: For larger categories, create subcategories based on specific characteristics or criteria.

Storage Solutions for Different Items

Finding suitable storage solutions is crucial for keeping your items organized, protected, and easily accessible. Consider the following options:

1. Clothing and Textiles: Hang clothing on sturdy hangers or fold them neatly and store them in labeled bins or storage containers. Consider using garment racks or installing shelves for efficient storage.

2. Small Items and Accessories: Use small bins, boxes, or organizers with compartments to store smaller items like jewelry, accessories, or small electronics. Clear containers or labeled drawers can make it easier to locate specific items.

3. Furniture and Larger Items: If you've found furniture or larger items, dedicate a designated space in your home or storage area for their storage. Consider covering them with protective sheets or blankets to prevent damage.

Managing Inventory and Keeping Track of Your Finds

Effective inventory management is essential for staying organized and maximizing the potential of your finds. Consider the following tips:

1. Create a Digital or Physical Inventory: Maintain a detailed inventory of your finds, either in a digital spreadsheet or a

physical notebook. Include item descriptions, condition, estimated value, and any additional notes.

2. Labeling and Tagging: Use labels, tags, or stickers to identify items and their categories. This makes it easier to locate specific items and keep track of your inventory.

3. Regular Inventory Assessments: Regularly review your inventory to assess the progress you've made, identify items that need attention (cleaning, repairs, or selling), and update the value of items based on market trends.

By implementing effective sorting and categorizing strategies, finding suitable storage solutions for different items, and implementing inventory management techniques, you can stay organized and maximize the potential of your dumpster diving finds. This ensures that you can easily locate items when needed, prioritize tasks effectively, and maintain a clear overview of your inventory.

Chapter 16: Space Requirements for Selling Online

If you plan to sell your dumpster diving finds online, it's important to consider the space needed to store and organize your items effectively. In this chapter, we will explore how to assess the space requirements for selling online, determine storage size for different types of products, and utilize shelves, hangers, and other storage tools effectively.

Assessing the Space Needed for Storing and Organizing Items for Online Selling

Before diving into the world of online selling, it's crucial to assess the space available to store and organize your items. Consider the following factors:

1. Available Space: Measure the space you have in your home, garage, or storage area that can be dedicated to storing your inventory. Consider both floor space and vertical space, as utilizing height can help maximize storage capacity.

2. Storage Capacity: Evaluate the storage capacity of the furniture, shelves, or storage systems you currently have. This will give you an idea of how much inventory you can accommodate.

3. Accessibility: Ensure that the storage area is easily accessible, allowing you to retrieve items efficiently when they sell or when you need to update inventory.

Determining Storage Size for Different Types of Products

Different types of products have varying storage requirements. Consider the following guidelines when determining the storage size needed for your items:

1. Clothing and Soft Goods: Clothing items can be stored efficiently on hangers, in bins, or in folded stacks. Assess the number of clothing items you have and the space required for their storage based on their sizes and bulkiness.

2. Electronics and Small Appliances: Consider the size and fragility of electronics and small appliances. These items may require additional protective packaging or specialized storage containers to prevent damage.

3. Furniture and Large Items: Furniture and larger items may need dedicated floor space or designated storage areas. Consider the dimensions of these items and plan storage accordingly to prevent damage or overcrowding.

Utilizing Shelves, Hangers, and Other Storage Tools Effectively

To optimize your storage space, utilize shelves, hangers, and other storage tools effectively. Consider the following strategies:

1. Vertical Storage: Install shelves or use stackable storage units to make use of vertical space. This helps maximize storage capacity while keeping items organized and easily accessible.

2. Hangers and Racks: Utilize hangers and garment racks to store clothing items efficiently. Consider using cascading hangers or space-saving hangers to optimize closet space.

3. Clear Containers and Labeling: Store items in clear containers to easily identify and locate specific items. Label containers or use clear sleeves to insert labels for quick reference.

4. Storage Systems: Invest in storage systems designed for specific items, such as jewelry organizers, accessory trays, or storage bins with compartments. These systems help keep smaller items organized and prevent them from getting lost or damaged.

By assessing your available space, determining storage size for different types of products, and utilizing shelves, hangers, and other storage tools effectively, you can create an organized and efficient space for storing and organizing your items for online selling. This will enable you to streamline your selling process and provide a positive experience for your customers.

Chapter 17: Choosing the Right Vehicle for Dumpster Diving

Having the right vehicle for your dumpster diving activities can greatly enhance your efficiency and convenience. In this chapter, we will explore the factors to consider when evaluating the ideal vehicle size for dumpster diving, the different options available such as cars, vans, or trucks, and how to maximize space and ensure convenience when transporting your finds.

Evaluating the Ideal Vehicle Size for Dumpster Diving

The size of your vehicle plays a crucial role in determining the amount and size of items you can transport. Consider the following factors when evaluating the ideal vehicle size for dumpster diving:

1. Payload Capacity: Check the payload capacity of the vehicle, which refers to the maximum weight it can safely carry. Consider the average weight of the items you typically find and ensure that your vehicle's payload capacity is sufficient to accommodate them.

2. Interior Space: Assess the interior space of the vehicle, including the trunk or cargo area. Consider the dimensions

and volume of the items you usually find to ensure they can fit comfortably within the vehicle.

3. Seating Configuration: If you often dive with a partner or a team, consider the seating configuration of the vehicle. Ensure there is enough seating capacity to accommodate everyone comfortably while leaving sufficient space for the items you collect.

Considering Car, Van, or Truck Options Based on Your Scale of Work

Different types of vehicles offer distinct advantages depending on the scale of your dumpster diving activities. Consider the following options:

1. Cars: Cars are suitable for smaller-scale diving or when space limitations are not a significant concern. They are generally more fuel-efficient and easier to maneuver in urban areas. However, their cargo space is limited, so you may need to be selective about the items you collect.

2. Vans: Vans offer a balance between cargo space and maneuverability. They provide more interior space than cars and can accommodate larger items. Vans with removable seats or cargo vans with an empty interior are particularly suitable for diving purposes.

3. Trucks: Trucks provide the most cargo space and are ideal for larger-scale diving or when collecting bulky items. They offer the flexibility to transport furniture, appliances, and other sizable finds. However, they may be less fuel-efficient and more challenging to maneuver in congested urban areas.

Maximizing Space and Ensuring Convenience When Transporting Finds

To make the most of your vehicle's space and ensure convenience during transportation, consider the following strategies:

1. Use Storage Solutions: Utilize storage bins, boxes, or containers to keep smaller items organized and prevent them from rolling around during transit. This also allows for easier unloading and sorting when you return home.

2. Utilize Tie-Downs and Straps: Secure larger or heavier items using tie-downs, bungee cords, or cargo straps to prevent them from shifting or falling during transit. This ensures both your safety and the protection of your finds.

3. Folding Seats or Removable Partitions: If your vehicle has folding seats or removable partitions, utilize this feature to create more space for larger items or to accommodate different load sizes.

4. Plan Efficient Routes: Plan your driving routes strategically to minimize travel time and maximize the number of diving locations you can visit. This reduces the need for excessive driving and optimizes your time and fuel efficiency.

By evaluating the ideal vehicle size for dumpster diving, considering car, van, or truck options based on your scale of work, and implementing strategies to maximize space and ensure convenience during transportation, you can enhance your diving experience and effectively transport your finds. Choosing the right vehicle ultimately contributes to your efficiency, productivity, and overall enjoyment of the dumpster diving process.

Chapter 18: Optimal Times for Dumpster Diving

Knowing the optimal times to go diving can increase your chances of finding valuable items and reduce the likelihood of encountering empty or picked-over dumpsters. In this chapter, we will explore how to identify the best times of the day to go dumpster diving, consider seasonal considerations, and explore peak diving opportunities during holidays and post-holiday seasons.

Identifying the Best Times of the Day to Go Dumpster Diving

Choosing the right time of day for dumpster diving can greatly impact your success. Consider the following factors when determining the optimal times:

1. Store Closing Hours: Visit dumpsters after stores have closed for the day. This increases your chances of finding discarded items from that day's operations or after restocking activities.

2. Early Morning: Check dumpsters in the early morning before businesses or

individuals have a chance to clear out the waste. This can be particularly fruitful for finding discarded items from the previous day.

3. Trash Pickup Schedules: Research and understand the trash pickup schedules in the areas you plan to dive. Visit dumpsters after the pickup has occurred, ensuring that new items may have been discarded.

Seasonal Considerations and Advantages of Specific Months

Different seasons can affect the availability and types of items you may find while dumpster diving. Consider the following seasonal considerations:

1. Spring and Summer: During these seasons, people engage in spring cleaning, move to new residences, or clear out old items. Take advantage of these periods to find discarded furniture, household items, and outdoor equipment.

2. Fall and Winter: The holiday season and the post-holiday period can be lucrative for dumpster diving. Many people dispose of unwanted or outdated items, providing an opportunity to find valuable items such as electronics, decorations, and clothing.

Peak Dumpster Diving Opportunities during Holidays and Post-Holiday Seasons

Holidays and the post-holiday seasons offer unique opportunities for fruitful dumpster diving. Consider the following:

1. Christmas: After Christmas, dumpsters near retail stores may yield discarded holiday decorations, unsold inventory, or returned items.

2. New Year: Dive near party supply stores or restaurants after New Year's Eve to find leftover party supplies, unopened champagne bottles, or disposable tableware.

3. Moving Days: College move-in and move-out days, typically at the beginning and end of semesters, can result in discarded furniture, electronics, and other items near student housing or university campuses.

4. Seasonal Clearances: Take advantage of post-season sales and clearances to find discounted items that retailers may be discarding to make room for new inventory.

By identifying the best times of the day to go diving, considering seasonal considerations, and exploring peak diving opportunities during holidays and post-holiday seasons, you can strategically plan your dives and increase your chances of finding valuable items. Remember to always follow local regulations, respect private property, and maintain safety precautions during your dives.

Chapter 19: Efficiently Packing Your Vehicle

Efficiently packing your vehicle is crucial for maximizing space, ensuring the safety of your finds during transportation, and maintaining an organized system for unloading and sorting. In this chapter, we will explore strategies for organizing and arranging items in your car or van, maximizing space while ensuring safety, and tips for securing and protecting your finds on the go.

Strategies for Organizing and Arranging Items in Your Vehicle

Effective organization and arrangement of items in your vehicle can help optimize space and prevent damage during transit. Consider the following strategies:

1. Categorize and Group: Sort items into categories and group them together. For example, place clothing items in one area, electronics in another, and furniture or larger items separately.

2. Utilize Storage Bins or Boxes: Use sturdy storage bins or boxes to contain and organize smaller items. Label them clearly to easily identify their contents.

3. Stack and Layer: Stack items of similar sizes and shapes to make the most of the available space. Place larger or bulkier items at the bottom and stack smaller items on top.

Maximizing Space while Ensuring Safety During Transportation

Maximizing space is essential when packing your vehicle for dumpster diving hauls. Consider these tips to make the most of your available space:

1. Utilize Vertical Space: Stack items vertically whenever possible to take advantage of the height in your vehicle. Secure taller items to prevent them from tipping over during transit.

2. Fill Empty Spaces: Fill gaps and empty spaces with smaller items or padding materials like blankets or pillows. This prevents items from shifting and helps maintain stability.

3. Secure Heavy Items: Place heavy items close to the vehicle's center of gravity and secure them using tie-downs, bungee cords, or cargo straps. This ensures they stay in place and do not create an imbalance.

Tips for Securing and Protecting Your Finds on the Go

It's crucial to secure and protect your finds to prevent damage during transportation. Consider these tips:

1. Use Protective Wrapping: Wrap delicate items in bubble wrap, packing paper, or blankets to provide cushioning and protection against bumps or vibrations.

2. Secure Fragile Items: For fragile items, use padding materials such as foam inserts or packing peanuts to minimize movement and absorb shocks.

3. Secure Loose Items: Use bungee cords, cargo nets, or cargo barriers to secure loose items and prevent them from shifting or falling during transit.

4. Protect Against Weather Conditions: If you anticipate inclement weather, use tarps or waterproof covers to protect your finds from rain, snow, or excessive sunlight.

By implementing strategies for organizing and arranging items in your vehicle, maximizing space while ensuring safety during transportation, and securing and protecting your finds on the go, you can streamline your packing process, optimize space utilization, and ensure the safe arrival of your dumpster diving hauls.

Chapter 20: Planning and Navigating Dumpster Diving Locations

Planning and navigating dumpster diving locations strategically can greatly enhance your efficiency and success in finding valuable items. In this chapter, we will explore how to develop a system for choosing and exploring different areas, researching potential dumpster diving spots, creating a route plan, and balancing variety and efficiency when determining which areas to visit and when.

Developing a System for Choosing and Exploring Different Areas

To make the most of your diving expeditions, it's important to develop a system for choosing and exploring different areas. Consider the following factors when selecting diving locations:

1. Variety of Businesses: Choose areas that offer a diverse range of businesses, as this increases the chances of finding a variety of items. Consider locations with grocery stores, retail outlets, apartment complexes, restaurants, and office buildings.

2. Local Knowledge and Recommendations: Tap into local knowledge by connecting with experienced dumpster divers in

your area. They can provide insights and recommendations on the best spots to explore.

3. Scouting New Areas: Continuously scout and explore new areas to expand your knowledge of potential diving spots. Keep an eye out for new businesses, construction sites, or residential areas undergoing renovations, as they may present opportunities for valuable finds.

Researching Potential Dumpster Diving Spots and Creating a Route Plan

Before embarking on your diving journey, research potential dumpster diving spots and create a route plan. Consider the following steps:

1. Online Research: Utilize online resources, such as forums, blogs, and social media groups, to gather information on potential diving spots. Look for tips and recommendations from other divers in your area.

2. Local Regulations: Familiarize yourself with local regulations regarding dumpster diving. Some areas may have restrictions or specific guidelines that you need to be aware of to avoid legal issues.

3. Map Exploration: Use online maps or physical maps to identify potential diving locations in your area. Mark them

down and categorize them based on the types of businesses or establishments present.

4. Route Planning: Plan your driving route based on proximity and efficiency. Consider the distance between diving spots, traffic patterns, and any time constraints you may have.

Balancing Variety and Efficiency When Determining Which Areas to Visit and When

When planning your diving trips, it's important to strike a balance between variety and efficiency. Consider the following factors:

1. Variety of Items: Aim to visit a mix of locations that offer a variety of items. This increases your chances of finding valuable and interesting discoveries.

2. Time Constraints: Consider the time you have available for diving. If you have limited time, prioritize locations that have a higher likelihood of yielding valuable items.

3. Day and Time: Certain days and times may be more favorable for dumpster diving, such as after store closing hours or on specific days when businesses tend to discard items.

4. Seasonal Considerations: Take into account seasonal variations in dumpster diving opportunities. For example,

during spring cleaning or holiday seasons, certain locations may have a higher likelihood of yielding valuable items.

By developing a system for choosing and exploring different areas, researching potential diving spots, creating a route plan, and balancing variety and efficiency, you can optimize your diving expeditions and increase your chances of finding valuable treasures during each trip.

Chapter 21: Making Dumpster Diving Enjoyable

Dumpster diving is not just about finding valuable items and saving money; it can also be an enjoyable and fulfilling activity. In this chapter, we will explore strategies for enhancing the enjoyment of dumpster diving, building a sense of adventure and exploration, and connecting with other dumpster divers to share experiences and learn from one another.

Strategies for Enhancing the Enjoyment of Dumpster Diving

1. Embrace the Sense of Adventure: Approach dumpster diving with a sense of adventure and curiosity. Embrace the thrill of the unknown and the excitement of uncovering hidden treasures. View each dive as a unique opportunity to discover something valuable or interesting.

2. Adopt a Positive Mindset: Maintain a positive attitude during your diving expeditions. Focus on the potential rewards and the joy of finding items rather than dwelling on any disappointments. Remember that dumpster diving is a unique and unconventional activity that allows you to make exciting discoveries.

3. Appreciate the Sustainable Aspect: Embrace the sustainability aspect of dumpster diving. Recognize that by rescuing discarded items, you are contributing to waste reduction and environmental preservation. Appreciate the impact you're making by finding new uses for items that would otherwise end up in landfills.

Building a Sense of Adventure and Exploration

1. Explore New Areas: Venture beyond your usual diving spots and explore new areas. Visit different neighborhoods, business districts, or even neighboring towns or cities. This not only adds variety to your dives but also allows you to discover new treasures in unexplored locations.

2. Try Night Diving: Consider exploring dumpsters during nighttime hours. Night diving can provide a different experience, with fewer people around and a unique atmosphere.

Take appropriate safety precautions and ensure good visibility with a flashlight or headlamp.

3. Document Your Finds: Keep a journal or take photos of your most memorable finds. Documenting your discoveries allows you to reflect on your diving experiences and create a visual record of the unique items you've rescued.

Connecting with Other Dumpster Divers and Sharing Experiences

1. Join Dumpster Diving Communities: Look for local or online communities of dumpster divers. Engage in discussions, share tips and experiences, and learn from the experiences of others. Building connections with fellow divers can enrich your own diving journey.

2. Attend Meetups or Events: Check for dumpster diving meetups or events in your area. These gatherings provide an opportunity to meet like-minded individuals, share stories, and learn new techniques or diving strategies.

3. Share Your Finds: Celebrate your finds by sharing them with others. Share items with friends, family, or members of your local community who might find value in them. Spread the joy of dumpster diving by gifting or donating items you don't need.

By implementing strategies to enhance the enjoyment of dumpster diving, building a sense of adventure and exploration, and connecting with other divers, you can turn dumpster diving into a fulfilling and exciting activity. Remember to always prioritize safety, respect local regulations, and approach each dive with a positive and open mindset.

Chapter 22: Choosing the Right Location for Dumpster Diving

Choosing the right location for dumpster diving is essential to maximize your chances of finding valuable items and to ensure a productive and safe diving experience. In this chapter, we will explore the factors to consider when evaluating the pros and cons of

living in large cities versus smaller towns for dumpster diving, assessing the availability of opportunities and competition in different areas, and considering factors such as population density, local businesses, and waste management practices.

Evaluating the Pros and Cons of Living in Large Cities versus Smaller Towns for Dumpster Diving

> 1. **Large Cities:**

> - **Pros:**

> - Higher population density: Large cities typically have a larger population, which means more businesses and potentially more discarded items to find.

> - Greater variety of businesses: Large cities offer a wide range of businesses, including retailers, restaurants,

universities, and more. This diversity can lead to a greater variety of items available for diving.

- More frequent turnover: With higher population density and a faster pace of life, there may be more turnover in terms of discarded items, providing more opportunities for finds.

- **Cons:**

- Increased competition: More divers in large cities can lead to increased competition for valuable items, making it more challenging to find treasures.

- Increased regulations and security: Larger cities may have stricter regulations and security measures in place, making it important to understand and abide by local laws.

2. Smaller Towns:

- **Pros:**

- Less competition: Smaller towns often have fewer divers, which means less competition for valuable items and potentially more fruitful diving experiences.

- Strong sense of community: In smaller towns, building relationships with local businesses and residents may be easier, fostering a sense of community and potentially opening up more opportunities for dumpster diving.

- Accessible diving spots: Smaller towns may have more accessible diving spots, as dumpsters are often in closer proximity to residential areas and businesses.

- **Cons:**

- Limited variety of businesses: Smaller towns typically have a smaller number of businesses compared to larger cities, which can limit the range of items available for diving.

- Potential limited availability: With fewer businesses, there may be fewer opportunities for diving, and finding valuable items may require more effort and persistence.

Assessing the Availability of Opportunities and Competition in Different Areas

When choosing a diving location, assess the availability of opportunities and the level of competition. Consider the following factors:

1. Number and Type of Businesses: Evaluate the number and diversity of businesses in the area. Look for locations with a variety of retail stores, restaurants, residential complexes, and universities, as these can provide a greater chance of finding valuable items.

2. Local Waste Management Practices: Research the waste management practices in the area. Some municipalities may have stricter regulations or more efficient waste disposal systems, impacting the availability of items in dumpsters.

Considering Factors such as Population Density, Local Businesses, and Waste Management Practices

1. Population Density: Consider the population density of the area. Higher population density generally translates to more businesses and potentially more discarded items to discover.

2. Local Businesses: Look for areas with a mix of businesses, including retail stores, restaurants, and offices. The more diverse the business landscape, the greater the potential for finding a variety of valuable items.

3. Waste Management Practices: Learn about the waste management practices in the area. This includes understanding trash pickup schedules, recycling initiatives, and any specific regulations related to dumpster diving.

Compliance with local regulations is crucial to maintain a positive relationship with businesses and authorities.

By carefully evaluating the pros and cons of living in large cities versus smaller towns, assessing the availability of opportunities and competition, and considering factors such as population density, local businesses, and waste management practices, you can make an informed decision about the best location for your dumpster diving endeavors. Remember to always respect local regulations, maintain good relationships with businesses, and approach each dive with curiosity and an open mind.

Chapter 23: Increasing the Value of Dumpster Finds

While dumpster diving can yield valuable items, there are ways to increase the value of the items you find. In this chapter, we will explore techniques for cleaning, polishing, or repairing items to increase their value, tips for restoring or repurposing found items for resale or personal use, and the importance of presentation and packaging in maximizing the perceived value of items.

Techniques for Cleaning, Polishing, or Repairing Items to Increase Their Value

1. Cleaning:

- Research Proper Cleaning Methods: Before cleaning an item, research the appropriate cleaning methods for the material or item type. Different materials may require specific cleaning agents or techniques.

- Use Gentle Cleaning Products: Opt for gentle cleaning products to avoid damaging delicate items. Avoid harsh chemicals unless necessary.

2. Polishing:

- Determine the Appropriate Polishing Technique: Consider the material of the item and research the suitable polishing technique. For example, metal items may require polishing with specialized metal polish, while wooden items may benefit from gentle sanding and varnishing.

- Invest in Quality Polishing Products: Use high-quality polishing products and tools to achieve the best results. This may include polish compounds, polishing cloths, or polishing machines.

- Follow Proper Application Techniques: Follow the instructions provided with the polishing products and use the appropriate application technique for the specific item.

3. Repairing:

- Assess the Repair Needs: Determine the extent of the item's damage and assess if you have the skills or resources to repair it. Consider factors such as broken parts, loose hinges, or missing components.

- Seek Professional Assistance if Needed: For complex repairs or valuable items, it may be advisable to seek the help of a professional restorer or repair specialist. They can provide expertise and ensure the item is repaired properly.

Tips for Restoring or Repurposing Found Items for Resale or Personal Use

1. Evaluate the Potential: Consider the condition and value of the item you find. Determine if it can be restored or repurposed for resale or personal use.

2. Research Restoration Techniques: If an item is in poor condition, research restoration techniques specific to the material or item type. This may involve repairing or replacing damaged parts, refinishing surfaces, or reupholstering.

3. Explore Repurposing Ideas: Look for creative ways to repurpose found items. For example, an old wooden door can be transformed into a unique tabletop, or vintage fabric can be used to create new clothing or home decor items.

The Importance of Presentation and Packaging in Maximizing the Perceived Value of Items

1. Clean and Arrange Items Nicely: Ensure that items are clean, well-arranged, and visually appealing.

2. Use Quality Packaging Materials: When selling or gifting items, invest in quality packaging materials. This may include boxes, tissue paper, bubble wrap, or ribbon. Proper packaging enhances the overall presentation and protection of the item.

3. Take High-Quality Photographs: If selling items online, take high-quality photographs that showcase the item's features and condition. Good photography can attract potential buyers and increase the perceived value of the item.

By implementing techniques for cleaning, polishing, or repairing items, exploring restoration or repurposing opportunities, and prioritizing presentation and packaging, you can significantly increase the value of the items you find through dumpster diving. Remember to always handle items with care, research appropriate techniques for specific materials, and have fun with the process of transforming and maximizing the potential of your finds.

Chapter 24: Costs and Expenses in Dumpster Diving

While dumpster diving can be a cost-saving and potentially profitable activity, it's important to consider the potential costs and expenses involved. In this chapter, we will explore the various aspects of costs and expenses in dumpster diving, including understanding the potential costs, budgeting for protective gear, cleaning supplies, storage solutions, and transportation, and balancing costs and potential profits to ensure a sustainable and profitable endeavor.

Understanding the Potential Costs in Dumpster Diving

1. Protective Gear: Investing in appropriate protective gear is crucial for ensuring your safety while dumpster diving. This may include gloves, sturdy shoes, safety goggles, and a reflective vest. Research and budget for quality gear to protect yourself from potential hazards.

2. Cleaning Supplies: Cleaning found items may require various cleaning supplies, such as detergents, brushes, and disinfectants. Consider the cost of these supplies when budgeting for your diving expenses.

3. Storage Solutions: Depending on the quantity and types of items you find, you may need storage solutions to organize

and store your treasures. This could include shelves, bins, or storage containers. Factor in the cost of storage solutions to keep your finds organized and protected.

4. Transportation: Consider the cost of transportation when planning your diving expeditions. This includes fuel costs, vehicle maintenance, and any parking fees that may be incurred. Determine the average distance you'll travel and estimate the associated costs accordingly.

Budgeting for Protective Gear, Cleaning Supplies, Storage Solutions, and Transportation

1. Assess Your Diving Needs: Evaluate the specific gear, supplies, storage solutions, and transportation requirements based on your diving goals and the types of items you anticipate finding. This will help you determine the appropriate budget for each category.

2. Research Costs: Conduct research to determine the average costs of protective gear, cleaning supplies, storage solutions, and transportation in your area. Compare prices from different vendors to find the most cost-effective options.

3. Prioritize Essential Items: Identify the essential items you need initially and prioritize them in your budget. This ensures that you have the necessary gear, supplies, and storage solutions to begin your diving adventures.

Balancing Costs and Potential Profits to Ensure a Sustainable and Profitable Endeavor

1. Set a Budget: Establish a budget for your dumpster diving activities. Determine how much you are willing to spend on gear, supplies, storage, and transportation without compromising your financial stability.

2. Track Expenses: Keep track of your expenses related to dumpster diving. This helps you stay within your budget and identify any areas where you may need to adjust spending.

3. Evaluate Potential Profits: Continuously assess the potential profits you can generate from selling or repurposing the items you find. This will give you an idea of the return on investment and help you determine if dumpster diving is financially viable for you.

4. Adapt and Adjust: Be prepared to adapt and adjust your budget based on the actual costs and profits you encounter. As you gain experience, you will have a better understanding of the financial dynamics of dumpster diving and can refine your budget accordingly.

By understanding the potential costs, budgeting for protective gear, cleaning supplies, storage solutions, and transportation, and balancing costs and potential profits, you can ensure a sustainable and profitable dumpster diving endeavor.

Remember to regularly reassess your budget and make adjustments as needed to maintain a financially responsible approach to dumpster diving.

Chapter 25: Profitability and Savings in Dumpster Diving

Dumpster diving not only allows you to find valuable items but also offers opportunities for profitability and significant savings. In this chapter, we will explore the potential financial benefits of dumpster diving, estimating monthly savings on grocery items and everyday essentials, and factors that affect profitability, including the quantity and quality of finds, selling platforms, and market demand.

Exploring the Potential Financial Benefits of Dumpster Diving

1. Cost Savings on Grocery Items: One of the primary financial benefits of dumpster diving is the ability to save money on groceries. By finding edible food items that are still in good condition, you can significantly reduce your food expenses.

2. Savings on Everyday Essentials: Dumpster diving extends beyond food. You can find a wide range of everyday essentials, including clothing, furniture, electronics, and household items, which can save you money on purchasing these items at retail prices.

Estimating Monthly Savings on Grocery Items and Everyday Essentials

1. Track and Calculate: Keep a record of the items you find and their estimated value. Calculate the retail prices of these items to determine the monthly savings you achieve through dumpster diving. This exercise can give you a clear idea of the financial impact of your diving efforts.

2. Assess Quality and Usability: Consider the condition and usability of the items you find. Some items may require minor repairs or cleaning, but their overall value can still be significant.

Factors that Affect Profitability in Dumpster Diving

1. Quantity and Quality of Finds: The more valuable items you find, the higher your potential profitability. Focus on diving in areas that consistently yield quality finds and target businesses that are more likely to discard valuable items.

2. Selling Platforms: Choose the most suitable platforms to sell your items based on their value, target audience, and convenience. Online platforms like eBay, Etsy, and Craigslist offer broad reach, while local markets and thrift stores may be better for certain items.

3. Market Demand: Consider the demand for the items you find. Research trends and identify niche markets that may be interested in specific categories of items, such as vintage clothing or collectibles.

4. Developing Selling Skills: Enhance your selling skills by learning about effective marketing techniques, pricing strategies, and customer engagement. The better you become at selling, the more profit you can generate from your finds.

The profitability in dumpster diving can vary depending on various factors, including the location, time invested, and the effort you put into selling your finds. It's essential to assess the potential savings and profits against the time and resources you dedicate to dumpster diving to ensure a financially viable and sustainable endeavor.

Chapter 26: Relaxation and Maximizing Energy for Dumpster Divers

Introduction:

Engaging in dumpster diving can be physically and mentally demanding, requiring energy, focus, and resilience. In this chapter, we will explore the importance of self-care and relaxation for dumpster divers, balancing work and personal well-being. We will also delve into various strategies to maximize energy levels and maintain a healthy mindset throughout your dumpster diving journey.

Section 1: Mindful Practices for Relaxation

1. Incorporating Meditation and Breathing Exercises into Daily Routines:

- Learn and practice meditation techniques to calm the mind and reduce stress. Regular meditation can enhance focus and bring about a sense of inner peace.

- Utilize deep breathing exercises to release tension and promote relaxation. These exercises can be done anywhere, providing instant relief during stressful moments.

2. Engaging in Mindfulness Activities to Reduce Stress and Increase Focus:

- Practice mindfulness in your daily life by bringing full attention to the present moment. Engage in activities such as mindful eating, walking, or simply observing your surroundings.

- Participate in activities that promote relaxation and self-expression, such as journaling, painting, or playing a musical instrument. These activities can serve as outlets for stress relief and personal reflection.

3. Exploring Relaxation Techniques such as Yoga, Tai Chi, or Nature Walks

- Engage in yoga or tai chi, which incorporate gentle movements and deep breathing to promote relaxation and physical well-being.

- Spend time in nature by taking walks in parks, forests, or along the beach. Connecting with the natural environment can have a rejuvenating effect on the mind and body.

Section 2: Physical Exercise for Energy and Stamina

1. The Benefits of Regular Physical Exercise for Dumpster Divers:

- Engage in regular physical exercise to improve energy levels, stamina, and overall well-being.

- Choose exercises that suit your preferences and fitness level, such as walking, jogging, cycling, or strength training.

2. Designing a Workout Routine that Fits Your Schedule and Preferences:

- Assess your schedule and determine the best time to incorporate exercise into your routine. It could be early mornings, evenings, or breaks between diving sessions.

- Establish attainable objectives and progressively enhance the intensity and length of your exercise sessions. This ensures a sustainable and enjoyable fitness regimen.

3. Engaging in Activities that Enhance Stamina, Strength, and Flexibility:

- Include cardiovascular exercises to improve stamina, such as running or swimming.

- Incorporate strength training exercises, such as weightlifting or bodyweight exercises, to build muscle strength and endurance.

- Remember to incorporate flexibility exercises such as stretching or yoga into your routine to enhance your range of motion and reduce the risk of injuries.

Section 3: Pursuing Hobbies and Interests

1. Identifying and Nurturing Personal Hobbies and Interests Outside of Dumpster Diving:

- Discover activities that bring you happiness and aid in relaxation. This could include hobbies like painting, playing a musical instrument, gardening, or cooking.

- Carve out dedicated time for your hobbies to ensure a healthy work-life balance.

2. Exploring Creative Outlets like Art, Music, or Writing:

- Engaging in creative pursuits can provide an outlet for self-expression and relaxation. Experiment with different artistic mediums, musical instruments, or writing styles to find what resonates with you.

- Join local art or music groups, workshops, or writing communities to connect with like-minded individuals and foster creativity.

3. Participating in Social or Community Activities to Foster Connections and Relaxation:

- Engage in social or community activities that align with your interests and values.

This could include volunteering, joining clubs or organizations, or participating in community events.

- Connecting with others who share similar passions can provide a sense of belonging and contribute to overall well-being.

Section 4: Continuous Learning and Skill Development

1. Expanding Knowledge and Skills in Areas Related to Dumpster Diving:

- Read books, blogs, or attend workshops that offer insights into the world of dumpster diving. Continuously educating yourself can enhance your expertise and boost your confidence in this endeavor.

- Stay updated on industry trends, new techniques, and regulations that may impact your diving experiences.

2. Exploring New Areas of Interest that Complement Dumpster Diving, such as Sustainability or Upcycling:

- Expand your knowledge beyond dumpster diving by exploring related areas of interest. This could include sustainability practices, upcycling projects, or learning about environmental conservation.

- Developing a broader understanding of these topics can enrich your diving experiences and contribute to a more holistic approach to waste reduction.

Section 5: Rest and Recharge

1. The Importance of Quality Sleep and Rest for Physical and Mental Well-being:

- Prioritize getting sufficient sleep to allow your body and mind to rejuvenate. Aim for seven to eight hours of uninterrupted sleep each night.

- Establish a consistent sleep routine by going to bed and waking up at the same time each day. Create a sleep-friendly environment that is cool, dark, and quiet.

2. Establishing a Healthy Sleep Routine and Creating a Comfortable Sleep Environment:

- Avoid stimulating activities, caffeine, or electronic devices close to bedtime. Instead, engage in relaxing activities like reading, taking a warm bath, or practicing a bedtime meditation.

- Invest in a comfortable mattress, pillows, and bedding to create a sleep environment that promotes restful sleep.

3. Incorporating Relaxation Techniques before Bed to Improve Sleep Quality:

- Wind down before bed by practicing relaxation techniques such as deep breathing, gentle stretching, or listening to calming music.

- Consider implementing a bedtime routine that signals to your body it's time to relax and prepare for sleep.

By incorporating mindful practices, engaging in physical exercise, pursuing hobbies and interests, continuously learning and developing skills, and prioritizing rest and relaxation, you can maximize your energy levels, maintain a healthy mindset, and ensure a balanced approach to dumpster diving. Taking care of your well-being enhances your overall dumpster diving experience and supports your long-term engagement in this rewarding activity.

Chapter 27: Building a Supportive Dumpster Diving Community

Dumpster diving doesn't have to be a solitary endeavor. In fact, building a supportive community of fellow divers can enhance your experience, provide valuable resources, and foster a sense of camaraderie. In this chapter, we will explore the benefits of connecting with fellow dumpster divers, finding or creating local groups and online communities, and sharing tips, experiences, and resources to build a strong network.

The Benefits of Connecting with Fellow Dumpster Divers

1. Knowledge and Information Sharing: Interacting with other divers allows for the exchange of valuable knowledge, tips, and tricks. Learn from their experiences and share your own insights to collectively enhance everyone's diving skills.

2. Emotional Support and Encouragement: Engaging with a community of like-minded individuals can provide emotional support and encouragement during challenging times. Fellow divers understand the ups and downs of the activity and can offer advice and motivation.

3. Safety and Security: Dumpster diving can sometimes be a risky endeavor, especially when diving alone. Being part of a

community provides an additional layer of safety. Diving with others can deter potential threats and ensure help is available if needed.

Finding or Creating Local Groups, Forums, or Online Communities

1. Local Dumpster Diving Groups: Research local dumpster diving groups or organizations in your area. These groups often organize diving events, meetups, and workshops. Joining these groups can connect you with experienced divers and help you discover new diving spots.

2. Online Dumpster Diving Forums and Communities: Explore online platforms dedicated to dumpster diving. Join forums and communities where divers discuss their experiences, share finds, and offer advice. These online spaces can be a treasure trove of knowledge and connections.

3. Social Media Groups: Search for dumpster diving groups on social media platforms such as Facebook, Reddit, or Instagram. These groups allow divers to connect, share photos of finds, and engage in discussions. Participating in these groups can broaden your network and keep you informed about the latest diving trends.

Sharing Tips, Experiences, and Resources

1. Participate in Discussions and Ask Questions: Engage in conversations within your chosen communities. The more you contribute, the more you'll benefit from the collective wisdom of the community.

2. Share Diving Spots and Insider Knowledge: Be open to sharing your favorite diving spots with trusted community members. By exchanging information, you can help others discover new fruitful locations, and they may reciprocate by sharing their own finds.

3. Organize Meetups and Diving Excursions: Take the initiative to organize diving meetups and excursions. These events provide an opportunity to connect with divers in person, exchange stories, and build lasting friendships.

4. Collaborate on Projects and Initiatives: Pool resources and knowledge with fellow divers to undertake collaborative projects. This could include organizing charity drives with found items, conducting educational workshops, or creating upcycling initiatives.

Building a supportive dumpster diving community requires active participation, open communication, and a willingness to share resources and knowledge. By connecting with fellow divers, both locally and online, you can create a strong network that enhances your diving experience, promotes safety, and fosters a sense of belonging within the dumpster diving community.

Chapter 28: Incorporating Sustainability into Dumpster Diving

Dumpster diving inherently aligns with principles of sustainability by reducing waste and promoting resourcefulness. In this chapter, we will explore the environmental impact of dumpster diving, tips for reducing waste and promoting sustainability in everyday life, and creative ways to repurpose or upcycle found items.

Exploring the Environmental Impact of Dumpster Diving

1. Waste Reduction: Dumpster diving helps divert items from ending up in landfills, reducing the overall waste generated by society. By rescuing and repurposing discarded items, divers contribute to a more sustainable approach to consumption.

2. Resource Conservation: Dumpster diving promotes the efficient use of resources by giving new life to items that would otherwise be discarded. By reusing and upcycling found items, divers help conserve materials and reduce the need for new production.

Tips for Reducing Waste and Promoting Sustainability in Everyday Life

1. Practice Conscious Consumption: Adopt a mindset of mindful consumption by considering the necessity and longevity of items before purchasing them. Make informed choices, opt for sustainable and ethically produced goods, and support local businesses that align with your values.

2. Embrace Minimalism: Reduce clutter and excessive consumption by adopting a minimalist lifestyle. Focus on quality over quantity and prioritize experiences and relationships over material possessions.

3. Reduce Single-Use Items: Minimize the use of single-use plastics and disposable products. Choose reusable alternatives such as water bottles, coffee cups, shopping bags, and utensils.

4. Compost Organic Waste: Start composting organic waste to divert it from the landfill. Use compost to nourish your garden or donate it to community gardens.

Creative Ways to Repurpose or Upcycle Found Items

1. DIY Projects: Use your creativity and crafting skills to transform found items into unique and useful creations. Repurpose furniture, create art from salvaged materials, or turn clothing into trendy fashion pieces.

2. Upcycling Household Items: Give new life to discarded household items by repurposing them for different purposes. For example, transform glass jars into storage containers or turn old pallets into unique furniture pieces.

3. Repair and Restore: Instead of discarding broken or damaged items, learn basic repair techniques to fix them. Restoring and repairing items not only extends their lifespan but also reduces waste.

4. Donate or Share: If you come across items that you don't need but are still in good condition, consider donating them to local charities, shelters, or community centers. You can also share them with friends, family, or neighbors who might find them useful.

By incorporating sustainable practices into your dumpster diving journey and everyday life, you contribute to a more environmentally conscious and responsible lifestyle. Reducing waste, promoting resourcefulness, and repurposing items not only benefit the planet but also inspire others to adopt more sustainable habits.

Chapter 29: Overcoming Challenges and Obstacles

While dumpster diving can be a rewarding and profitable activity, it is not without its challenges. In this chapter, we will explore common challenges faced by dumpster divers and provide strategies for overcoming them. By understanding and proactively addressing these obstacles, you can enhance your diving experience and increase your chances of success.

Common Challenges Faced by Dumpster Divers

1. Unfriendly Encounters: Occasionally, you may encounter individuals who are unsupportive or hostile towards dumpster divers. This could be due to misconceptions, personal biases, or concerns about liability. Dealing with such encounters requires tact and resilience.

2. Negative Reactions: Some people may not understand or appreciate the value of dumpster diving, leading to negative judgments or comments. Overcoming negative reactions requires confidence in your chosen activity and the ability to educate and inform others respectfully.

3. Scarcity and Competition: Dumpster diving spots can become crowded, especially in areas with high diving activity. Competition for valuable finds and limited resources can be a

challenge. It requires adaptability and creativity to navigate through scarcity and find alternative sources.

Strategies for Overcoming Challenges and Obstacles

1. Educate and Raise Awareness: Educate others about the benefits of dumpster diving, its environmental impact, and the potential for finding valuable items. By sharing information and dispelling misconceptions, you can help change attitudes and foster understanding.

2. Develop Strong Communication Skills: Enhance your communication skills to effectively engage with individuals who may be skeptical or hostile towards dumpster diving. Use facts, personal experiences, and empathy to address concerns and misconceptions.

3. Foster Positive Relationships: Build relationships with business owners, security personnel, and other individuals who may have influence over dumpster diving access. Establishing a positive rapport can lead to more amicable encounters and increased access to diving locations.

4. Seek Legal Knowledge: Familiarize yourself with local laws, regulations, and property rights pertaining to dumpster diving. Understanding your rights and responsibilities will help you navigate legal boundaries confidently and avoid potential conflicts.

5. Stay Motivated and Resilient: Dumpster diving can be physically and emotionally challenging at times. Cultivate resilience by focusing on the positive aspects of the activity, celebrating successes, and learning from setbacks. Surround yourself with supportive individuals who can uplift and motivate you during challenging times.

6. Diversify Your Diving Locations: Explore a variety of locations beyond traditional spots to diversify your opportunities. Consider areas such as construction sites, university campuses, or residential neighborhoods to increase your chances of finding valuable items.

7. Develop Alternative Skills: Diversify your skill set to enhance your diving success. Learn about upcycling, repairing, or refurbishing found items to increase their value. Acquire knowledge in specific areas of interest, such as antiques or electronics, to identify valuable items more effectively.

By employing these strategies, you can overcome common challenges and obstacles encountered in dumpster diving. With resilience, effective communication, and adaptability, you can navigate through unfriendly encounters, negative reactions, competition, and scarcity. Challenges are opportunities for growth and learning, and with persistence, you can achieve success in your dumpster diving endeavors.

Chapter 30: Conclusion - Embracing the Dumpster Diving Lifestyle

In this final chapter, we arrive at the end of our enlightening exploration of dumpster diving. Throughout this book, we have delved into the depths of dumpsters, uncovering the secrets and possibilities they hold. Now, as we bring this journey to a close, let us reflect on the lessons learned, the experiences gained, and the profound impact of embracing the dumpster diving lifestyle.

Throughout these pages, we have discovered that dumpster diving is not merely a means to save and make money; it is a gateway to a world of self-sufficiency, resourcefulness, and environmental consciousness. It is a way of life that challenges the norms of our consumer-driven society and encourages us to reevaluate our relationship with material possessions.

In our exploration of dumpster diving, we have shattered misconceptions and shed light on the legalities surrounding this practice. We have discussed the importance of safety, ethics, and responsible diving, ensuring that we approach this activity with mindfulness and respect for both the environment and the communities we encounter.

We have learned to maximize our dumpster diving hauls, from sorting and valuing our finds to determining the best avenues for selling, donating, or repurposing them. We have explored the thrill of uncovering valuable items, from antiques to electronics, and recognized the potential for not only financial gain but also personal fulfillment in our discoveries.

Moreover, we have celebrated the freedom and flexibility that dumpster diving offers. We have embraced the joy of setting our own working hours, taking breaks when we desire, and experiencing the liberation that comes with being the masters of our own destinies. The dumpster diving lifestyle empowers us to chart our own course and create a balance between financial savings and personal enjoyment.

As we conclude this book, let us remember that dumpster diving is more than just a solitary pursuit. It is a community, a network of like-minded individuals who share a passion for exploration, sustainability, and the thrill of the hunt. By building supportive relationships with fellow divers, we create a space for knowledge sharing, inspiration, and camaraderie.

So, dear reader, as you embark on your own dumpster diving adventures, I urge you to carry the lessons and insights gained from this book in your heart. Embrace the surprises and challenges that come your way, for they are part of the journey. Cherish the treasures you find, whether they be material or intangible, and share the joy and knowledge with others who may be inspired to embark on their own diving expeditions.

As you navigate the dumpsters, the alleyways, and the hidden corners of the world, remember that dumpster diving is not simply about saving and making money. It is about forging a connection with the past, breathing new life into discarded objects, and reimagining the possibilities they hold. It is about making a positive impact on the environment, one dumpster dive at a time.

So, my fellow diver, go forth with courage, curiosity, and a sense of purpose. May your dumpster diving journey be filled with bountiful finds, meaningful connections, and personal growth. Embrace the dumpster diving lifestyle and let it guide you towards a path of self-discovery, fulfillment, and sustainable living.

Thank you for accompanying me on this transformative exploration of dumpster diving. May the wisdom gained within these pages empower you to embrace the beauty and potential that lie within the depths of the dumpsters. Remember, the world of dumpster diving is yours to explore, so dive deep and uncover the treasures that await.

The End

www.ingramcontent.com/pod-product-compliance
Lightning Source LLC
Chambersburg PA
CBHW062330290526
45794CB00005B/1979